CW00449150

HOW TO BE A BOMB
ANDY FLETCHER

HOW TO BE A BOMB
Andy Fletcher

ISBN 9781903110300
First published in this edition 2016 by Wrecking Ball Press.

Cover design by humandesign.co.uk
Typeset by leeds-ebooks.co.uk

the
James Reckitt
library trust

Supported using public funding by
ARTS COUNCIL
LOTTERY FUNDED   ENGLAND

Supported by
Hull UK City of
Culture 2017

CONTENTS

HOW TO BE A BOMB

wait
by a roadside
or in some grass

don't think
about who made you
or what their motives were

you know
that even the slightest touch
will mean the end of you
and not only you

hope
an unsuspecting soldier
steps wide of you

pray
a child's inquisitive fingers
stop
an inch away from you

CUSTODY

the piano's arrested
and charged with making people happy
together with the secondary offence
of encouraging them to sing

bail's refused
and the piano's taken into custody

the piano's legal representative
asks why the piano's been charged
when it can't play itself

she demands an explanation
as to the deep scratches
that have appeared on the piano's lid
why the soft pedal's broken
and some of the notes won't sound

in the silence that follows
music can be heard
coming from the cells

OVERCOATS

the sun's blazing down

tar's melting on the road

i meet you outside a shop
and stop to talk

you're wearing an overcoat

i say 'that looks nice and warm'

'yes' you reply 'it's thick
 and keeps out the cold'

you tell me
you like the overcoat i'm wearing
especially the fur trimmed collar

we're both red-faced and sweating
but we don't say a word about it

we look down the street

as the heat simmers
i notice
everyone's wearing an overcoat

OBITUARY

the italian film director almena finzione has died in naples at the age of ninety two. her most famous films include 'donkey on a teaspoon' and 'god runs off with the money'.

after quitting university without a degree finzione moved into the film business and it wasn't long before she persuaded the prestigious 'la burla' studios in rome to let her try her hand at directing. from her early work including 'naked congregation' and 'the quick production of mountains' (a winner at the cannes festival) she rapidly developed to produce the classic feminist polemic 'the woman who married a battering ram'. finzione herself never married and declared 'i am married to my art'.

from the breathtaking 'all traffic lights are green' with its attack on commercialism and the monotony of modern existence she continued in a rich vein throughout her thirties and forties causing outrage among church leaders and government ministers when her attack on colonial exploitation 'stroffinacio sovrano' ('imperial dishcloth') was released. finzione ever calm in a storm responded to the official fury by walking in a meditative pose non-stop for twenty four hours round the neptune fountain in florence.

critics generally acclaim 'the extraordinary baldness of lighthouses' as her masterpiece but her own favourite was her homage to personal and political freedom 'voluntary gold' though in an interview conducted in her eighties she cited 'sawing through the bars of a blue headache' as a film that despite 'incredible difficulties' in its making (shot high in the pyrenees in the worst winter for forty years) had acquired 'a certain resonance' in its completed form.

although finzione had a reputation for being able to drink most men under the table it is for her lucidity and transcendence that she will be remembered. moments such as those immortalised in her autobiographical swansong 'ricordo dentale' ('dental souvenir') where in a fascinating sequence she compares destiny to a piece of chocolate slowly melting on a windowsill in the sun. we will not see the likes of her again.

REMAKING HISTORY

the americans
decide to remake history
by dropping
on hiroshima
not an atomic bomb
but candles

instead of a mushroom cloud
towering above
instead of buildings
resembling black lace
there's a different outcome

one that doesn't say
'we hate you'
'we want to annihilate you'

but says
'you're the same as us'

although
the pilot reports
'mission accomplished'
he doesn't add
'now i'm getting the hell out of here'

this time
he circles round
and looks down
at millions of tiny lights winking up at him

I WAKE UP NEXT TO YOU

i wake up next to you

overnight you've become fifty years older

your hair that was dark brown when you switched out the light
has become silvery grey

your face is suddenly lined and wrinkled

last night you stripped off and almost dived into bed but now
you say your back's hurting your joints are aching and you'll
need help to get up

your voice has changed too

you ask me to assist you to the bathroom but before we get
there you urinate on the floor

in the mirror i glance at myself

i look and feel no different from yesterday

when i pass you a tissue i notice several of your teeth are
missing

you ask me if i remember saying i'd always love you when we
lay in each other's arms last night

'yes' i say slowly 'yes i do'

THE ATLAS

we used to read the atlas together

you said
'an atlas can take you anywhere
the more you look the more you see'

you pointed at a river
a frontier
a peninsula i'd never heard of

sometimes you'd lean closer to the pages
and i'd feel your breath on my hand

occasionally we'd make a few notes

at some point
we must have closed the atlas
not realising
we wouldn't open it again

the furthest you move now
is from one side of the bed to the other

a peninsula everyone knows about

as the nurse
writes on a sheet of paper in a file
your breathing is shallow and fast

the more i listen the more i hear

FATHER AND SON

all your life
when we met
you'd shake my hand

it always felt
as if you were concluding
a business deal

now as you lie in bed
semi-conscious
and close to death
i wonder how you might be feeling
about me stroking your cheek
and smoothing back your hair

BLACKING OUT

i black out
a word
a phrase
a sentence

i black out
a paragraph
a whole page

what it takes to destroy
what it takes to get free

the blacking out means
nothing of what was written
can be read

what it takes to love
what it takes to forgive

THE SPEAKING HORIZON

the speaking horizon
says
'honour your parents'

the speaking horizon
says
'respect your neighbours'

we decide to go out
in our little boat
and see where the voice is coming from

as we row
we hear it saying
'put your litter in the bin provided'

soon
the coast is out of sight
but we still seem to be no nearer
to where the sound is coming from

'keep off the grass' we're told
'leave the exit clear at all times'

no matter how hard we row
the speaking horizon
always maintains its distance

'stand clear of the platform edge'
the voice continues

'make sure you lock your doors and windows'

suddenly we realise
we've got no food and no water
suddenly we realise
we've got no compass

FIRE STATION

what happens if the fire station were to catch fire?

well that should be quite simple
the firefighters would drive the fire engines out a few metres
and turn the hoses on the blaze

but what if the fire engines were out on a call?

well the station manager would have to ring the next fire station
and get them to send their team

but what if the next team were also at a fire?

well the fast response auxilliary vehicle would have to be called out
and that would tackle the job

but what if all the engines
and the auxiliary vehicle were busy
and the telephone wires had been cut
and the workers left at the station had switched off their mobiles?

well the cleaner would have to run out into the street
and ask a passer-by to contact the police

but what if the cleaner had cramp in her legs
or had fallen asleep after lunch?
and what if the passer-by forgot
or the police had all been sent to a major crowd disorder

well then it would come down
to the fire station's emergency sprinkler system

but what if the sprinkler system
hadn't been filled or had frozen
or there was a power cut because of fallen lines
or someone had accidentally drilled through a cable
so there was no electricity
and the sprinkler sensors weren't activated?

well then in that case the fire station would go up in flames

THE BLUE HOUSE

the walls are painted blue

the roof is painted blue

the door is painted blue

the windows
even the glass
are painted blue

people who see the house say
it's absurd
stupid
mad
crackers
weird
senseless
potty
bizarre
ridiculous

no one ever forgets the blue house

THE BENCH

the waves on the estuary are twinkling and rippling and the leaves of a tree are doing the same. north korea detonates a nuclear test device. you said you didn't want to be with me any more. lichen has grown on the bench. a day is a long time. i thought i could save the situation but i couldn't. the blast measures 4.7 on the richter scale. a white butterfly flutters over the grass. there are cracks in my trainers i haven't noticed before. anyone can come along and sit on the bench. the suncream i'm wearing is the same as the one you used to rub over your body. i glance up. glittering might be a better word to describe the waves. people talk to each other across thousands of miles. we can't talk to each other in the same room. the nuclear test is in contravention of security council resolution 1718. the litter bin has its own shadow. does emotional closeness depend on physical closeness? it's easy to get obsessed with loss and what we haven't got. the explosion took place six miles underground. you said 'it's all so superficial'. paint on a railing has flaked off. the shadow of a litter bin is the same whatever the colour of the bin. the prime minister says the koreans actions are 'misguided and a danger to the world'. you claim i'm no good for you. the sky has not a cloud in it. vaporized people leave only shadows.

INTERNATIONAL

england flags
fly from our french and german cars
built with components from indonesia
and fuelled by petrol
refined from saudi arabian or iraqi oil

we support a team
half of whose players are of african
or caribbean extraction

we wear shirts made in taiwan
trainers manufactured in thailand

we yell at our japanese televisions
run on electricity generated in wales
by burning polish or russian coal
imported on bulgarian ships

we pull open cans of dutch and belgian beer

to celebrate a win or for consolation in defeat
we go to a chinese
or indian restaurant for a curry
or order a pizza from an italian takeaway

waiting for the kick-off
of the spain v australia match
i whistle a tune by the american band the dixie chicks
and check the time on my swiss made digital watch

A LADDER LEANING AGAINST A WALL

it drives her mad
the way she has to do
everything for him

even the small things about him
annoy her
the way he picks at his scalp
and makes it bleed

some days
she'd like to throw the cut glass vase
and watch it smash against the wall

as if doing that might mean
he could walk by himself again
and say 'i'm fine i can do it'

so that he might
come over to where she's sitting weeping
and put his arms around her

CARPETS

we're sitting at home
watching tv
when the carpet starts to undulate
and groan

a few minutes later
it gives birth to a mat

'how on earth has that happened?'
my mother asks

my father replies
'i reckon it's something to do
with the carpet in the hall'

the little mat
is an orangey colour
and everyone wants to touch it

'there could be commercial possibilities
in this' says my brother
'think of all the money we could make
selling mats'

'you're right' my father agrees
'why don't we leave the carpets
to get on with it?'

we pack up and go off
for a fortnight's holiday

on our return
we're hoping to find
the house full of mats

when we get back
there's still only one

my mother sighs
'oh well that's how it goes'

we stand around not saying much
just looking at the little orange coloured mat

SPLIT

from north to south
the country cracks in half

a ravine
runs through the capital
and people stand and stare
across the divide

speculation mounts
as to whether
the split's been caused
by tensions
between
rich and poor
young and old
black and white

working flat out
day after day
trucks arrive
to pour concrete
into the gap

as workers smooth
the top layer
the prime minister
congratulates the nation
on its efforts
and declares the country to be
'as good as ever'

just then
there's a rumbling
and another huge crack appears
this time
from east to west

THE LOVERS

she was hot and horny she was hungry she was all the 'h's' including heresy and hair she was heave-ho and hooting

and as for the dark it was lined it was layered it was lathered it was for letting go and leaping it was lava it was a leech it was lager and loopy it was luxurious and lollipop it was a lunar locomotive

and the air inside the car was stifling as they took off their clothes it was shark infested and syrupy it was starlit and steepled it was supple and stereophonic it was a swarm a surge a see-saw a scrum it was sausagey and sticky it was shaved and strong it was salty and full of swearing

THE WAY I FEEL ABOUT YOU

like the roses
that have climbed a fence

and tumbled over
to bloom on the other side

HEAT

the window wide open

your hand stroking my arm

my hand touching your hair

the flowers in the vase
can no longer keep their scent to themselves

THE DAM

from the hillside
we look down at the reservoir
at the huge wall of the dam

we've walked through bracken
we've ducked under branches

you've been talking about dinosaurs
about the great sweep of history

i point to the little tower
where measurements are taken

millions of gallons of water

a collapse of the wall
could make our hearts beat faster
and start the drowned trees
breathing again

maybe
the dam is the government
the system
anything that holds us back
from who we can be

all those feelings

i take your hand
and squeeze it

gazing at the dam
i realise what's pent up
what's waiting to be released

imagine

the joy
cascading

DEAD TREES

we're in our cabin on the ferry. you're listening to music i'm reading a book. the word 'decision' takes me back to a meeting i attended. what's heard what's not heard? the manager told the meeting that although marjorie had been 'prim and proper' all her life she was now coming out with 'foul' language and 'improper' suggestions and upsetting the other residents. are different thoughts put in different compartments? maybe there are cabins in my head. down on the bottom bunk you're whistling along to a song. everything's fine until proven otherwise. our coats hang on pegs side by side. what happened yesterday can seem a long time ago. we'd stopped and looked at some dead trees that had been painted various colours including orange green and blue. you take out your earphones and say 'are there any of those flapjacks left?' the tree that was painted white had a startled look and was the one that unsettled me. the manager said marjorie had started wrapping her faeces in paper and hiding them in her wardrobe. what's seen what's not seen. you said the purple tree should have had plums on it. is our thinking due to chance? A friend chuckled as he recalled his daughter secreting birthday chocolates inside her socks in a drawer. who decides what's right and wrong? i'd noticed how birds seemed to shun the painted trees. A woman once told me she'd love me 'for ever and ever'. did anyone say that to marjorie? what happened years ago can seem like it happened yesterday. who decides what's real and what isn't? as the ferry engines rev up the bedside lamp rattles and water in a bottle shakes. we'd walked beyond the dead trees and as we looked up there must have been a hundred or more birds perched and singing on a high voltage wire.

BIG FIELD

a big field
reaching almost
as far as i can see

in my hand
is the letter you've sent

i fold the single sheet of paper

i fold it again
and again
until it becomes so small
and hard
i can't fold it anymore

the big field
i must remember
the big field

COWS WILL FLY

the house of commons is full of cattle

electoral success has packed the chamber
with friesians and jerseys ayrshires and herefords

'order order' cries the speaker

the front benches resound with masticating
and the swishing of tails
(quite different from the tales we used to hear)

a live broadcast is for once
perfectly intelligible
with sounds of not more than one syllable

shit splatters the carpets
and buttercup leads a stampede into the lobbies

grass for all!
the abolition of slaughter houses!
dairies to be consigned to diaries!

no longer will cows be used for
shoes and handbags

above the river thames
castles in the air take on the shape
of cattle in the air
proclaiming a new era of democracy

ANNA

all that's left
is a drop of water
on a polished table

LIVING IN A HOUSE THAT HASN'T YET BEEN BUILT

i'm living in a house
that hasn't yet been built

everyone i tell says it's impossible

show us the house they say
show us the bedrooms the lounge the kitchen
they say

i shrug my shoulders

i carry on living
in a house that hasn't yet been built

MY UNHAPPINESS

i give my unhappiness a cup of tea
i give it a twenty pound note
and a recording of a nightingale

i enrol my unhappiness on a course of basket weaving
i send it for a week on a silent retreat
i send it for several sessions with a psychotherapist

i let my unhappiness ride round a corner no-handed
i let it climb to the top of a sycamore and throw twigs at me
i let it fly to tenerife and lie in the sun

i take my unhappiness and buy it a new car
i take it out for a slap-up meal
i take it to a bar and let it get paralytically drunk

i threaten my unhappiness   i plead with it
i humour my unhappiness   i whisper to it
i stroke it   i give it a pep talk

my unhappiness looks back at me like a small child

THE HUT

the boss jim thorpe threw open the door to our hut.

mike and i should have been working but we'd stopped for a tea break and not started again. and now it was nearly lunch time. mike was a surveyor in charge of me his chainman. we should have been out measuring for the next part of the new motorway me holding the pole and mike looking through his theodolite.

during our tea break mike had told me he was a buddhist and that he'd gained great insights from his practice of meditation and how he'd realised there was a spiritual dimension to living 'far beyond these things'. as he talked i looked at the rough wooden walls of the hut and wondered about my karma and what my destiny would be. mike had just started explaining about everlasting peace when the door to the hut flew open.

'what the fuck do you think you're doing?' jim thorpe shouted. 'we were just about to get started' mike replied. 'about to about to what bloody use is that?' said jim thorpe. 'you're out mate down the fucking road'. 'and you' he said turning to me ' get back to base'.

mike picked up his bag and walked off. i climbed into the land rover that would take me back to the base.

and though i saw many rough wooden walls after that i never again saw mike nor heard any more about everlasting peace.

A MAN TAKES OVER A RAILWAY STATION

a man takes over a railway station. he changes the station's name and sacks the staff who work there. he increases the charges for train operators to use the station. the amount of passenger traffic dwindles rapidly. before long there's only the occasional freight train passing through. the man decides these are too noisy and has all the signals switched to red. he blocks off the station entrance so that only he can use the subway climb the footbridge and walk to the ends of the platforms. now there's not the clink of a coupling nor the hoot of a horn to be heard. he looks at the rusty tracks and smiles.

BOB SMITH

there appeared flotsam
and a grey seal
experimenting with sunlight.
oh and the non-stop pumping of the bilges.
i could not fully control the result.
the silver of the sea sagged
as bob smith arrived from below deck.
seeing him i couldn't help but think
of a loofah or a scrubbing brush
and how essential the unconscious is
in the face of evidence to the contrary.
'i never touch a drop' said bob
wagging his finger which accidentally
drew attention to the flash of a bottle
sailing away behind him
bobbling beyond the grey seal
some seaweed and a jutting rock
which reminded me of our good captain's nose.
standing above bob and me on the bridge
he was just possibly a saint
though peeling a banana
reduced his saintliness by a few degrees.
'blood and saliva we're all made of the same'
said bob 'life is pretty simple really'.
'it would be' i replied 'if you've never
 sailed a ship through a force ten gale'.
'clarity will come' said bob
but his face was beginning to sweat
from wrestling with so many concepts.
coming down to join us

the captain laughed loudly
'why everything's a question of observation'
he said pointing to three seagulls in our wake.
'each one of those birds
 is a floating village of ticks and mites'
he added with a chuckle
'as their beaks will find out'.
and we gripped the deck rail a little tighter
watching the horizon rising and falling.

YOU AND ME

i stare
at the remains of the jetty

buckled rails
proud rusty nails with nothing fastened to them
charred and hanging timbers

around it all
the water swirls

BLENDER

you're listing my failings
and telling me
there's so much i've done wrong

i watch you
loading the clear plastic drum of the blender
with walnuts
pieces of bread
chunks of onion
and oil

you slot on the lid
secure it
and press the button

you continue to tell me
how i haven't loved and respected you

staring at the blender
and its whirling contents
i see the flashing of the stainless steel blade

NOTEBOOK

standing on the deck of the ferry i realise i've lost my notebook. i left it either at the cafe or in the lodgings. you've checked your bag. i've checked mine. recorded and unrecorded life. the language of looking. i hold on to the deck rail. the notes from a holiday when we walked the coast. was it raining? the language of not knowing. is it important? is it the present or the past that matters? the notebook's gone. the language of connection. a man in a high visibility jacket on the deck tosses a line to a man in a high visibility jacket on the jetty. the notes will probably end up in a landfill site or an incinerator. the language of the past. a winch squeals and up out of the river comes a big chain. bits of mud drop from it as it's pulled tight. the language of the moment. the links make shadows on the water.

THE 3-LINE-STANZA SPECIAL

after receiving
a number of queries and
comments regarding the feasibility

of a residents
parking scheme for mount
pleasant and being handed a

petition
i have now arranged for
an open meeting with mr k

allenby
the lead officer at the borough
council and the person

behind the
excellent bankside scheme
who can detail the

pros and cons
explain the
finances and answer any questions

POLICE STATE

we roll down a slope laughing

the grass is flattened and then springs up again

we reach the bottom and run back to the top

down the slope once more we go laughing and rolling

james worked on the typing all that day. he'd been neglecting it but it was the one thing he could do for dana and it would keep his mind occupied. dana came home after dark. it was still raining and she looked haggard. she took off her muddy boots on the verandah, went to the bathroom to wash, then came straight to the dining table for her meal. she ate in silence and barely glanced at james sitting opposite her in his long-sleeved chiffon shirt. he felt a fool for dressing up since dana was still in her work clothes, her hair tangled, her hands rough with hard labour. dinner over, james stacked up the dishes and determined he would ask dana some intelligent questions and put out a feeler in case there was some way he could help.

'i was wondering if i could be of some assistance, i mean, i...' he faltered, aware of her scepticism. 'so if there's anything i can do'.
'there's nothing' dana said shortly 'i wouldn't dream of asking you to ride out in the rain. the next thing you'd have pneumonia'.
'and i'm nuisance enough without that aren't i?' james broke in bitterly.
'you could say that' dana agreed, lighting a cigar.

the next morning james completed the typing. just before lunch he thought he heard the sound of dana's car and ran outside eagerly, thinking perhaps she had come back for him. but it wasn't dana, it was pete.
'hi jim' said pete 'i just called round to see if you fancy coming to the men's underwear party tonight?'
'no' said james quietly 'dana's not here and i can't go anywhere without her permission'.
'are you in love?' asked pete.

'deeply' replied james looking back at him through quivering eyelashes.

later that night during yet another storm, james was about to go to bed when he saw dana standing in the bedroom doorway. he felt a shiver go up his spine. he tried to push past her but she put out an arm to stop him, he allowed her to kiss him, to undo the buttons of his pyjamas. their bodies were so close and he knew that at any moment she would lift him up and carry him across to the bed and complete what she had started.

A SERIES OF DOTS

sometimes i throw away a day
as if it were an old cracked ornament

later my children come home
and say 'look what we've found'

and show me an old cracked ornament

DRAWER

i open your drawer
and find a baby crocodile inside

one with plenty of sharp teeth

it snaps its jaws
and i push the drawer quickly shut

you knew i wasn't to be trusted
when it came to your personal documents

now i'm not going to be able to read
what i want to read

and i'm going to have to keep quiet
about the crocodile

MORE THAN I CAN SAY

the sun coming through the window
doesn't wake you

the fine hairs on your bare arm
glisten

SHINDIG

she sits at her desk and replaces the handset.
'he's leading us all a shindig' she says.

'shindig' (1)

'a noisy party, dance etc'

'party' (2)

'a group of persons
joining together, taking
part in and approving of
or being aware of what
is going on'.

'dance' (3)

'to move with
measured rhythmic steps,
usually to music, to be
in lively movement, to
bob up and down'.

'aware' (4)

'having knowledge or
realisation'

'step' (5)

'the movement of the foot
or one foot after the
other'.

---

(1) nobody appears to be dancing. the situation doesn't in any way suggest a party, let alone a noisy one.

(2) can a party exist without anyone joining together?

(3) i remember a black man at a club who danced so slowly he could hardly be perceived to be moving at all.

(4) does anyone know or realise, or even know or realise that they know or realise?

(5) is it possible to dance without moving a foot or one foot after the other? see also (3)

i watch her at her desk and recall what she said –
'he's leading us all in a shindig'. (6)

---

(6) i know what she means. (c.f. notes 1-5).

GOLFERS

the golfers are playing in a war zone

a ball lands in a bomb crater

one of the golfers
selects a wedge and chips the ball out

when there's a missile attack
the golfers mark the spot where their ball is
and take shelter

after the raid they continue

if a green's destroyed
the golfers aim for where they think the hole should be

some children wander out onto the course
one on crutches
another with a bandaged head

the golfers shout
and wave to them to stand clear

nothing can stop the golfers
as they drag their trolleys over the battered ground
past a burned out tank

even the sight of the clubhouse
being blown to pieces
and putting paid to a gin and tonic after the game
does not deter them

ROAD RAGE

and when i've finished
calling him
a bastard
a fat bastard
just because
he cut me up in his 4 x 4 outside tesco's
i remember
my subscription to greenpeace
that i'm supposed to be a gentle person
that violence breeds violence
and i think instead
of the organic cabbage in my rucksack
and conjure up saint brassica
the bra-less saint of overtaking
and then i think i shouldn't be thinking about that either
only of carrier bags filled with wind
of my own hot air
a thin bastard
a thin aggressive bastard on a racing bike
and how i should try changing positions with fatso
bonnet up
ghosts hard as cauliflowers
coming out of the exhaust pipe

THE AFTER LIFE

i die
and head off to the next world
not to be served with curry
but presented with parcels
which when i unwrap them
have nothing inside

all except the last one
which contains a cassette
labelled
'the horse waltz'

ARMCHAIRS ON THE MUDFLATS

on the mudflats
we're sitting in armchairs

we're a family in a semi-circle
around the television

we're watching a cowboy film

our daughter says her chair
seems to be sinking into the mud

we tell her not to be concerned

our son says the tide's coming in

i reassure him
'don't worry it won't reach us'

seagulls wander over the mudflats
and there's a curlew as well
dipping its long beak

our son says
'the water's up round the telly now
don't you think we should go?'

'go where?' i reply
'this is our home'

the water begins to reach his chair

and rise up it
'look' he exclaims

'be quiet' his mother says 'you're spoiling the programme'

'my bottom's getting wet' our daughter complains

'will you two stop interrupting' i say
'we want to see if the sheriff comes to the rescue'

ONLY

only us
sitting on a beach watching
watching the tide come in
the tide come in
the water climbs
climbs the old black stumps of the groynes
soon
only the tips are showing
only the tips
and then there's only water
as it continues to rise
to rise
something's happening here
here with you
that's not only the water
the water
something in these moments
only in these moments
something sparkling
sparkling

SUNLIT

you look at me
and smile

i smile back

neither of us
seems to know what to say

beyond us
there are deep lines
in a field of wheat

THE SUSPENSION BRIDGE ACROSS YOUR OPEN HANDBAG

(a poem compiled from the following sources – the collins
scandinavian phrase book. elementary technical electricity by kt
agger. iron in the soul by jean paul sartre. the beano and modern
sociology by prof. t manslaughter)

the darkness is so white.
it's not what i expected
but then repulsion and attraction
seem much closer than i previously thought
and linked in some way i can't understand.
you light a cigarette.
it grows longer as you smoke it.
things are acting in such peculiar ways.
what is connected to what and what is that connected to?
it's no good saying 'get that cat gnasher'
or 'grrr you'll pay for this dennis'.
i shall never live this down or up.
or maybe it's all because my ears need syringing.
we want better quality not pass the parcel
especially when the parcel gives us an electric shock
but nothing behaves like it should any more.
the city's swung way out on its moorings.
expressions like 'phenomenological ethnomethodology'
need scrapping and replacing
with 'boing' and 'whee' and 'yee hee' and 'scrubba dubba dub'
there are many ways of breaking the law.
add another nought to the speed limit.
anything you want.
anything i want too.
i shop-lift a lamp that stays lit as i run down the street.

EDUCATING THE DEAD

skeletons are removed from coffins
and returned to a classroom
to be educated

the teacher instructs them
about the diesel engine and the petrol engine
about neutrons and electrons
about stars beyond the recognised solar system

the skeletons make excellent pupils
and their behaviour is exemplary

they don't answer the teacher back
and make no noise in class

they don't even want to go out into the playground
at break or dinner time

they enjoy learning so much
they sit all day at their desks
and never stop grinning

THE BIRDS OF POVERTY

the birds of poverty
rarely get off the ground

they're sometimes seen
under a bush
or at a kerb

the birds of poverty
congregate
in run down and industrial areas
and are seldom seen
in leafy suburbs

although politicians talk about
the birds of poverty
and how they need to be eradicated
they never disappear

all year round
their plumage is grey

the birds of poverty
are never seen flying

how could they
when they have no wings?

THE SEXUAL PLEASURE OF LEVEL CROSSINGS

the thrust
and whoosh of a train

then the opening of the gates
and the relaxation

and all the little thrills
of the traffic's rubber wheels
crossing over

THE EXPLANATION

your explanation's a long freight train

i count the trucks as it passes

each one's connected to the one in front
and seems to be another reason
for what you've done

the buffers are bumping
the wheels are squealing

i'm still trying to understand what you're telling me
as the red winking light on the last truck
disappears from sight

i hear the train clattering
over a metal bridge in the distance

I THINK OF THAT GIRL

when i push past the other drinkers
on my way to the bar
i think of that girl

when i listen to a joke
one of my workmates is telling
i think of that girl

when i look round
at people in their fashionable clothes
at them talking and laughing
i think of that girl

when the music starts
and i feel it in my body
as i start to dance
and people whoop and begin to shake their bodies too
i think of that girl

when i look out into the dark
where taxis are waiting to take us home
and the take-aways and restaurants
shine out on the street
i think of that girl

that girl
that indian girl
a company's negligence
a chemical explosion
her charred cheek
a red growth over her eye

THE POWER

you're rollerskating across the sea

away from what's probable
away from what's believable

your legs and arms drive you on
and spray flies up
as you feel the exhilaration of the wind

keep rollerskating
before your feet
turn to blocks of concrete

before the dead rise up out of the waves
and pull you down

SEX

the women in the office are talking about sex again.

the question's posed as to whether they'd sleep with the man of their dreams if there was no way their husband or partner could find out.

'a free shag' as ann puts it.

in her case it'd be george clooney. in delia's case robbie williams.

delia and ann say yes they definitely would.

linda however says no she wouldn't because she couldn't 'live with herself' though she wouldn't mind 'flirting' with the man of her dreams.

'cockteaser' says ann.

when sarah's asked she says she's given up sex and become asexual. someone thinks she means bi-sexual but she says 'no i've given up on it altogether'.

the others say 'i bet'.

i see the manager approaching down the corridor and say 'dave's on his way'. dave who probably isn't the man of any woman's dreams.

the women all resume typing on their keyboards.

'what's happening in here then?' dave asks.

'we're hard at it' says delia.

'it's non-stop' says ann.

'as always' says linda.

BROWN JACKET

your brown jacket's
embroidered with elephants
purple red and green

the jacket's missing several buttons
which you haven't bothered to sew back on
possibly because you've lost them

the jacket looks so right on you
it wouldn't seem wrong
to say the jacket is you

one day when you're not wearing it
i read the label
'100 % cotton'
'made in india'

there's a used tissue in the right hand pocket
there are two used tissues in the left

am i talking about the jacket
because really i'm wanting to talk about you
and how i feel about you?

here you are again in the jacket
a carnival of colour being worn by you
and carried into the world

your brown jacket
with all the elephants trumpeting

THAI SPRING ROLL AND PUSSYKINS

gaeng khieow waan gaeng panaeng pat mamuang himapar prieow boing waan kratiem prik pak ruam pat dtooa ngork miaow pah garee massaman gaeng supparot pat khing met mamuang himapar miaow outabag prik haeng pak tempura popia tort popia tort boing

GUITAR

an empty room. sunlight slanting across it. a guitar propped against a white painted wall.

you pick up the guitar. a plectrum inside. you try to shake it out. you shake out the person you were when you were young. before you can speak that person gets up off the floor pulls a face and vanishes.

tricks damned tricks.

it was your friend who wrote the songs. his hair tucked behind his ears. his fingers flowing over the strings. you could have practiced for years and never been able to do what he could do.

where is he?

he's not at the bottom of your beer bottle.

not inside a blister in a pack of codeine tablets.

why did you stop playing music?

people are wax melted
and gone hard again.

you could smash the guitar against the wall. smash it until the neck comes away from the body. smash for all that's twisted all that's lost for all that's dead and beyond.

you put down the guitar.

your shadow on the wall is shaking

SAFE AS HOUSES

i arrive home and put my key
in the door

a policeman's sitting behind a desk
in the hallway

'what are you doing here?' i ask
the policeman says he's making sure
no one enters the house illegally
and requests i show him my pass

'i'm the property owner' i say
pushing past him into the kitchen
where two policewomen are drinking mugs of tea

in the living room
more police with their hats and helmets off
are sitting round the television

'we're checking everything's secure' they tell me

upstairs
i find three members of the constabulary
in my bed

in the bathroom
one copper's in the shower
another's sitting on the toilet

'your home's as safe as the bank of england'
one of them says

i rush out of the house
not knowing where i'm going
out into the dark and windy night

AIR STRIKES

on a high speed train we're racing through england's green and
pleasant land

members of parliament have voted 524 to 43 in favour of air
strikes in iraq

a tractor harrowing a field is creating clouds of dust

a woman on her phone's saying 'come on it's a good excuse to
go out and celebrate'

the bombing endorsed by the archbishop of canterbury

we carry on reading newspapers magazines listening to music
on earphones looking at laptops tablets mobiles at some
sort of screen

'oh god'

the bodies will be someone's brother sister mother father friend

a warehouse security light's blazing in the middle of the day

'we'll go out for a meal and then meet up with the others in the pub'

establishing democracy and the fight against extremism

advertisements for luxury chocolates and luxury toilet rolls

the union jack flying from a tower

in a scrap yard a crane's lifting a car without wheels and
   placing it on top of a car without a bonnet

'it's a great opportunity to get together'

the bodies will be someone's aunt uncle daughter son

the archbishop's talking of 'a compelling vision'

the sound of a bag being zipped up

the train gives a blast on its horn that sends sheep running in
   all directions

the door's locked so no one can get off

in the middle of a field of stubble there's a dead tree

THE MOON

you're waving a stick at the moon

you keep jabbing at it
and eventually manage to knock it
to the ground

you start beating the moon with the stick

people try to restrain you
but you shake them off
and keep hitting

the moon's already losing its light
and is beginning to shrink

on the pavement
you stand panting
as the last of the light runs away down the drain

you look up at the empty sky

you throw down the stick
and start sobbing

MARCHING WALLPAPER

marching wallpaper
is advancing down the street

left right
left right

the marching wallpaper
enters through our front door
and fastens itself to the walls

'hey' i shout
'we don't want a floral pattern
in here'

you come down the stairs
and say 'now we've got paper
with flying ducks on it in the bedroom'

it turns out everyone down the street
is experiencing the same kind of thing

already it's being talked about
as 'the occupation'

some people have ripped down the wallpaper
but straightaway more's arrived to replace it

left right
left right

it's not only our street
but the whole city and country
that have been taken over

i open a box of matches
and strike one

we both stare at the flame

FLAG DAY

i'm standing on a street corner
rattling a can

i'm collecting for the rich
and in return for money
i'm giving people a little sticker
which reads 'i'm helping the rich'
to place on their lapels

an old woman comes up
puts a coin in the tin
and says 'i like to give to good causes'

a man asks me
'who is the money going to exactly?'

'only the richest' i reply
'you know the likes of dukes and duchesses
 bankers and tycoons'

'that's alright then' says the man
pushing a folded note into the slot

soon the can's feeling quite heavy

a woman with matted hair
a filthy coat and holes in the toes of her shoes
drops a coin in

she winks at me and says
'the rich need all the help they can get'

WATER

on the footbridge near the ferry terminal
water's dripping from a stanchion
and forming a large puddle on the metal landing

i'm thinking about you
and trying to decide
whether you're the dripping water and i'm the puddle
or the other way round
or both

whichever way
it doesn't end there

the water's overflowing from the puddle
and running down the next flight
step after step

DIRECTORY

social democracy	parrot
electoral reform	weak sunlight
elections	perfume
supreme court	blocked toilet
social security system	the handcuffs
individualism	protruding veins
roman catholic church	an angel a blindfold
socialism	big hill
inflation	stodgy pudding cleavage
anarchism	storm scattered birds
taxation	hamper hunger
civil service	layers of wallpaper
think-tank	poultry shed
nazism	room without light
traditional conservatism	dancing in a suit of armour
president	mud the trumpeter
revolution	deep breathing the blaze

VEHICLE CHECK

max breakforce left	pulse
max breakforce right	touch
wheel drag left	a smile
wheel drag right	a whisper
contact pressure	body on body
calculation pressure	lips and hair
ovality left	heart/mind
ovality right	exuberant skin
wheel weight left	quicker breathing
wheel weight right	quicker breathing
axle weight	fingers
side slip	sweat
wheel bind left	flesh tingling
wheel bind right	innermost feeling
efficiency against presented weight	groaning moaning shouting
efficiency against plated weight	god jesus holy mother
additional information (1)	lifted out and above
additional information (2)	extended fields

THE POLICE DRESSED IN BABIES' BONNETS

the police wearing babies' bonnets
don't arrest you
or ask you to move on

they don't take you in for questioning
or charge you with any offence

you may be apprehended
in an act of theft

you may be caught
with a gun in your hand
and a dead body at your feet

the police wearing babies' bonnets
stroke your hair
and sing to you

they're even offering you a bonnet
just like theirs

WOMAN ON A MOBILITY SCOOTER

the teenagers form a line across the pavement
so that when the woman on her mobility scooter reaches them
she has to stop

she asks politely if they'd mind
letting her through

gathering round her
they start rocking the scooter
as if it were a rowing boat

with a shout
they tip it on its side
and run away laughing
leaving her lying on the pavement

blessed are the merciful for they shall have mercy shown them
blessed are those who thirst for righteousness and justice for
    they shall be satisfied
blessed are the pure in heart for they shall see god

unable to get up
the woman looks at her overturned shopping
at the burst yolks from a couple of broken eggs
running slowly across the pavement towards her

MY CHILDREN

a piece of chipboard

a length of electrical wire and a plug

a number of light fittings
each containing a bulb
mounted on the chipboard

where are the dolls and teddy bears?
where are the crayons and story books?

the bulbs are lighting up
at random intervals

at any time
all the bulbs or none
or any combination of them may be shining

THE WAR ON TERROR

the war on terror
the terror of war
of warts and terriers
the territorial army
the war against wardrobes
the terror of wardrobes
hide inside and terrorise
with terrifying noises
like termites
or the warbling warden
locked in war
in war-like gestures
the war on socks
warm socks worn socks
a black sock hanging
from a shelter
at the terrible terminus
no terra firma
to fight the good fight
your own terror
revealed by wobbling
and excessive winking
until there's no such thing
as terminal terminology
as territory or terror
only the all-out assault
of the war on war

CLEANING THE WIND

the government's decided
the wind needs to be cleaned

companies are invited
to tender for the work

it's known the wind picks up
smoke
exhaust fumes
particles of soot
as well as the smells of industrial chemicals
and paint

the company which wins the contract
sets about trying to clean the wind
which is where the problems begin

where is the scaffolding to be erected
and the ladders to be leaned?

the cleaners find their blades and cloths
just sink into the air

'how do we know which parts of the wind
are dirty and which parts are clean?'
one of the workers asks

'this is harder than we thought'

SING

sing
for a smashed clock
for a roof without slates

sing
for a charred bookcase
for a wingless aeroplane

sing
for a rose that's lost its petals
for a grounded abandoned ship

sing
for madness for failure
for collapse for inertia for defeat

sing
for a dog that can't walk
for a rain-swollen bible

sing
for a window without glass
for a hand with missing fingers

sing
for disappointment for delusion
for error for waste for loss

sing
for a bus with no wheels
for a shell far away from the sea

sing
for a child lying in a crater
sing

HOUSE OF A THOUSAND ROOMS

on this unlit day
when dust is blowing round inside me
i settle into my gestapo niche

death to x
death to y
death to z

then just as i'm about to overwhelm myself
the bricks become soft
and i put on the musical gown of easy listening

now i'm a fat sultan
i superdeluxe me

CREATIVITY

in a small room
you sink into the plush upholstery

there with his arm around you
is a sweaty wrestler
you could never have imagined meeting

BROTHER

you're looking at me

can you see me?

i'm the brother
who has only part of a face

my mouth has been nibbled in the reeds

your fingers move over my skin
over what remains

i don't expect you to understand
and how could you?

you're not to blame in any way

i looked at the dark water
at lights spinning on the surface

eventually i jumped
and felt myself being handed
from one current to another

you place your ear
to what's left of my lips

i've no voice

you may only hear
a hooter in the fog
sounding again and again

THE TAX ON BREATHING

a tax has been imposed on breathing

we stay indoors and try sitting still
to avoid incurring costs

under the new tax
walking isn't cheap
and running's prohibitively expensive

as for sex
the cost has become exorbitant

some people try
wearing motorcycle helmets and niqabs
so they can't be seen taking in the air
but everywhere
there are cctv cameras and breath sensors

we hear about people who can't pay
being put to sleep

we're terrified of a knock on the door
and seeing through the glass
a tax inspector with monitoring equipment

to think we used to jump and dance
to laugh and shout
to run towards the sea with our arms out wide

how did all this happen?

ACKNOWLEDGEMENTS

'bob smith' appeared in 'smile the weird joy' anthology (Ragged Raven press)

'shindig' appeared in *Bete Noire* 10/11

'notebook' appeared in *Poetry Salzburg* 17

'the hut' and 'the speaking horizon' appeared in *The Hull Connection* anthology (Muesli Jellyfish)

'the bench' appeared in *Poetry Salzburg* 21

'remaking history' and 'how to be a bomb' appeared in the Amnesty International anthology *Small Candles*

'the after life' and 'golfers' appeared in *Turbulence* 14

'road rage' appeared in *The English Chicago Review* 3

'armchairs on the mudflats' appeared in *10 miles East of England* booklet for Hull's 2017 City of Culture bid

'marching wallpaper' and 'the moon' appeared in *Poetry Salzburg* 27

'air strikes' and 'safe as houses' appeared in *Tears in the Fence* 62

'guitar' appeared on the dvd *moment* (Connell-Hunter) [attic 71/youtube]

'brother', 'cleaning the wind', 'the tax on breathing', 'woman on a mobility scooter' and 'water' are due to appear in *The Slab* 4

Many thanks for support and advice to Tony Petch, Frank Newsum and Mary McCollum.

BIOGRAPHICAL NOTE

Andy Fletcher was born in Halifax and now lives in Hull. He graduated in law but has since worked as a farm labourer, machine operator, bus driver and social work assistant. His poems have appeared widely in magazines including *Bete Noire, Tears in the Fence, Poetry Salzburg Review, Butcher's Dog* and *Iota*. He has been anthologised in *Old City New Rumours* (ed Carol Rumens/Ian Gregson), *The Hull Connection* (Muesli Jellyfish) and Amnesty International's *Small Candles*. His collection *the mile long piano* was published by Ragged Raven in 2007. Andy is an occasional vocal performer with experimental band 'Fear of Bicycles'.